A NOTE TO PARENTS

When your children are ready to "step into reading," giving them the right books—and lots of them—is as crucial as giving them the right food to eat. **Step into Reading Books** present exciting stories and information reinforced with lively, colorful illustrations that make learning to read fun, satisfying, and worthwhile. They are priced so that acquiring an entire library of them is affordable. And they are beginning readers with an important difference—they're written on four levels.

Step 1 Books, with their very large type and extremely simple vocabulary, have been created for the very youngest readers. **Step 2 Books** are both longer and slightly more difficult. **Step 3 Books,** written to mid-second-grade reading levels, are for the child who has acquired even greater reading skills. **Step 4 Books** offer exciting nonfiction for the increasingly proficient reader.

Children develop at different ages. **Step into Reading Books,** with their four levels of reading, are designed to help children become good—and interested—readers *faster*. The grade levels assigned to the four steps—preschool through grade 1 for Step 1, grades 1 through 3 for Step 2, grades 2 and 3 for Step 3, and grades 2 through 4 for Step 4—are intended only as guides. Some children move through all four steps very rapidly; others climb the steps over a period of several years. These books will help your child "step into reading" in style!

Library of Congress Cataloging-in-Publication Data:
Edwards, Roberta.   Five silly fishermen/by Roberta Edwards; illustrated by Sylvie Wickstrom.   p.   cm.–(Step into reading.
A Step 1 book) SUMMARY: A retelling of the traditional tale in which five silly fishermen, unable to count properly, are convinced
that one of their group has drowned.   ISBN: 0-679-80092-1 (pbk.); 0-679-90092-6 (lib. bdg.) [1. Folklore] I. Wickstrom, Sylvie
Kantorovitz, ill. II. Title. III. Title: 5 silly fishermen. IV. Series.   PZ8.1.E26Fi 1989   398.2′1–dc19   [E]   89-42508

Manufactured in the United States of America   24   25   26   27   28   29   30

STEP INTO READING is a trademark of Random House, Inc.

Step into Reading

Five Silly Fishermen

By Roberta Edwards
Illustrated by Sylvie Wickstrom

A Step 1 Book

Random House 🏠 New York

One fine day
five fishermen
went fishing.
One, two, three, four, five!
Down to the river they ran.

One sat on a rock.

One stood

on the dock.

One climbed

up a tree.

One lay in the grass.

And one fisherman
got into a boat.
"Hello, down there!"
he called to the fish.
"We are ready to catch you!"

At the end of the day
each fisherman had
a nice fat fish
on his line.

"What a fine supper
we will have!"
said one fisherman.
"Now let's go home."

"First we must count to see
if we are all here,"
said another.
"What if one of us
fell into the water?"

13

So he began to count.
"One, two, three, four.
I see four fishermen.

Oh, no!

One of us <u>is</u> missing!"

"It cannot be!"
said another fisherman.
"Maybe you counted wrong."

So he began to count.

''One, two, three, four.

I see four fishermen too!

It is true.

One of us has drowned!''

All the fishermen
hugged each other.
They cried and cried.
"Our poor friend!
What will we do
without him?"

19

Just then
a little girl came by.
She was going fishing too.
"Why are you so sad?"
she asked them.

"There used to be
five of us.
But one drowned,"
said a fisherman.
"Now there are only four.
See!
One, two, three, four,"
he counted again.

Well, right away
the little girl
saw his mistake.
The fisherman forgot
to count himself.

"Will you give me your fish

if I find your friend?"

she asked.

"Yes! Yes!" they said.

"Now jump into the river
one at a time,"
the little girl told them.
"And I will count you."

The fishermen did
as they were told.
Splash!
Into the river they went.

One!

Two!

Three!

Four!

Five!

"Five!"

the fishermen shouted.

"Our lost friend is found!

He did not drown after all!"

The fishermen
gave the little girl
all their nice fat fish.
Then home they went.

They were very wet.

They had no fish for supper.

But they were
all together again!